DAYS TO HIGHER PRAISE

We all need to start somewhere.

A devotional by
Jason Adams

90 Days to Higher Praise: We all need to start somewhere.

Published by E2V Coaching, LLC
Livonia, MI
Email: jason@e2vproject.org
Website: www.e2vproject.org
Text & Cover Design: Keigh Cox

ISBN: 978-1-7364484-0-3

TABLE OF CONTENTS

INTRODUCTION AND BREAKDOWN

Most books have introductions, so let me give you mine. This will help break down my thoughts and vision for the purpose of this book. I know that living a believer's life is hard, I know it is challenging, and I know that each day we miss building a life of praise and thanksgiving is just another day here on Earth. I am truly thankful for God's grace and mercy, because Heaven knows how many days, I've had that were just another day here on Earth and not used to connect with the Creator of the universe.

I wanted to write a book that is first: easy to use, and second: is direct and purposeful in helping to build an attitude and lifestyle of praise to the King of kings. I will say this, I am a reader, but it has been a habitual partaking in my life to get there. I read a lot as a kid, it subsided as a teen and young adult, but then my attitude towards learning and reading took a turn later in life, and I became a person who is dedicated to lifelong learning. In this book, I am hoping you'll glean some information from me as I have from others and use it to build a purposeful and dedicated life of praise and thanksgiving to the One who truly deserves it.

So, let's discuss how this book is going to be broken down. You'll only have to read, update, and journal a thought on ONE page a day! Yep! You are reading only one page. On each page, you'll start with simple tasks that ideally will take around fifteen to twenty minutes each day to accomplish. This time will increase as you are challenged to add a little more every ten days. For example, you will be starting off with five minutes of prayer and work up from there, but there may be days when five minutes are not cutting it. Things going on in your life may require thirty minutes of prayer, and so what - that's great!

The goal of this book is to help you build simple habits that ignite a daily interaction with God. We have all been hearing it for years, how important it is to have a daily walk with God and it is so vital. This book is NOT the answer to everything, and it is NOT a magical set of steps. It IS however a tool and technique that CAN direct you to a life CONNECTED to God, rather than just another day here on Earth.

The second part of the book breakdown is habit forming, we will attempt to slowly build in four key areas that I see help connect a believer with God daily. We will look at prayer, devotional time, Bible reading, and journaling. I can already hear you say, "How am I going to do all this in one day?" That answer is quite easy, I wrote the book so you can succeed in this daily task. How about if I give you a little secret here early on so that you are encouraged to move on? Most of the tasks you'll be doing will require you to put a check mark next to the assignment when completed. Yep! No multiple choice, no true or false, no deep diving into dictionaries or commentaries, none of that is required. The fact that this is broken down for you, is what I believe will help with the keys to success.

My hope and prayer for you is that you can take this 90-day book and create a lifestyle that will bring fulfillment, joy, and peace. So, are you ready to get started? Let's go!

FOUR CORE AREAS EXPLAINED

The first area each day will look at prayer. It will require a gradual gain of momentum to get you started on your new or improved prayer life. This book, being 90-days long, will take time moving into a more intense prayer life, but the good news is once prayer becomes habit it no longer becomes a task or a checkbox on the list, but an opportunity to have fellowship with God, and not because you have to, but because you want to. What a great thought! The idea is that we must start somewhere, so we are going to start off small and work our way up to more consistent and thorough prayers.

The second area each day is Bible reading. Again, this is a gradual build and I will be providing all the necessary Bible scriptures you'll use. At first it will be one or two scriptures, and as we grow, we will have you open the actual Bible and read a section for yourself. Don't worry! I believe in you and I know you can do it. The Bible is our lifeblood, our rulebook, and our communication tool with God. We, as believers, need to be equipped with its truth and we need to have it in our hearts and our spirits because as the days get tougher we need to be able to have something of sustainable peace in our lives.

The third area each day is devotional, which means "of or used for religious worship". I believe our lives are one area where we can please God and be a testimony for others to watch and learn to worship with us. So, devotional in this book will be a core thought, a way to apply truth, or a positive quote. It will provide you something to ponder on throughout the day and lead you to think of God more practically and openly. Far too many times we only see God as a rule enforcer, which He is, but He makes rules for our benefit, He enforces them in our best interest. If we only look at the King of kings as someone enforcing rules, we will fail to see how loving, merciful, and kind He really is. This is the purpose of the devotional section; it will make you think.

The fourth section is journaling. Okay, okay, I know you're already starting to freak out and wonder what I have in store for you here. What if I told you at the beginning your journaling requirement will simply be a sentence? Yes, that's it, a sentence. I will ask you to write a sentence of how your day went, or what impacted you most in your walk today, or how God gave you a new perspective on things. It really is used to draw attention to this super important person in God's life, and that's YOU. What did you get out of this tremendous blessing we call the present day, and as we grow throughout the book you'll be challenged to write more, maybe even leading up to a paragraph...? Who knows, by the end of this book you could be writing your own book. I really believe that could happen.

CHALLENGE CHANGES EVERY TEN DAYS

- **Days 1 – 10**: Just getting into a rhythm
- **Days 11 – 20**: We add a Bible verse
- **Days 21 – 30**: We add another Bible verse
- **Days 31 – 40**: We add some thanksgiving into your prayer time
- **Days 41 – 50**: We add the needs of a friend to your prayer time
- **Days 51 – 60**: We add your specific needs to your prayer time
- **Days 61 – 70**: We add a second sentence to your journaling assignment
- **Days 71 – 80**: We add another sentence making a paragraph to your journaling assignment
- **Days 81 – 90**: We add a chapter of Bible reading to your overall plan

THE HOW TO AND WHY OF THIS BOOK

I've read a lot, and I still do to this day. There has been a little less actual reading while I've spent time writing the books that I've been blessed to have pressed on my heart to write, but one of the best books I have read in a while has to do with leading yourself and creating habits for success. I am not going to go into quotes and breakdowns of other people's work, but I will recommend two books that have energized me to write this 90-day journey.

Lead Yourself First – Inspiring Leadership Through Solitude
By Raymond Kethledge & Michael Erwin

Quotes from the book

- Solitude is simply, a subjective state of mind, in which the mind, isolated from input from other minds, works through a problem on its own.
- Today's world puts too much emphasis on the immediate.
- Another way to obtain self-awareness is through reflection.

Jane Goodall, who wrote *Reason for Hope*, stated, "The first step on the road to experiencing true awareness is the cessation of noise from within." This quote as well as the quotes above from *Lead Yourself First* was one of the core reasons I decided to write this 90-day journey. We must get back to the simple things in life, we must get to our own personal center, and at that center we MUST have God. Some people will want to argue this point but nearing my 30-year mark in my walk with Christ I can honestly say that Him being at the center has made all the difference. Now let's look at book number two.

Atomic Habits – An Easy & Proven Way to Build Good Habits and Break Bad Ones
By James Clear

Quotes from the book

- Habits are not a finish line to be crossed, that are a lifestyle to be lived.
- You do not rise to the level of your goals. You fall to the level of your systems.
- Never miss twice. If you miss one day, try to get back on track as quickly as possible.

"So, this is how it's going to be," you may be thinking, and yes, that is exactly what I am saying. If we are going to be effective, I mean purposefully effective in the ministry and the missional commands of Christ we must develop a good habit of being aligned to the Master in our spirit, our mind, and our body. We need to carry truth with us, we need to have wisdom to share, and knowledge to stay enthused.

This is a daily journey. This is not a something you do and in 90-days you are done. Even though you'll be done with this book, the hope is that this will be a tool in your life toolbox and will give you the enthusiasm and drive to continue your daily journey with God. One more quote from James Clear to drive home the point, "Every action you take is a vote for the person you wish to become." Isn't that great? That was so motivating to me and was one of the reasons I wrote this.

SPECIAL THANKS AND ENCOURAGEMENT

So, I know that special thanks and stuff like that need to be at the beginning of the book, but I wanted it here, and since I'm the author, it's going here (insert sarcastic smile and raised eyebrow). I first and foremost want to thank my Lord and Savior Jesus Christ for making the ultimate payment for me and giving me real purpose here on Earth. I am forever grateful and forever changed. I want to thank my beautiful bride, April, for being my constant source of kindness and goodness in my life, you model these two wonderful attributes with excellence, thank you for teaching me to be less naughty. I thank my children Abigail and Hunter for allowing me time to write this book, serve in ministry, and be a dad all at the same time. Thanks for always being patient with me. Finally, thank you to my mentors Curt Dalaba, Dr. Dave Williams, and Dr. Keith Johnson for sharing your wisdom with me throughout the years. I am eternally grateful.

So now the encouraging part…This is the most you'll have to read to finish this book. Yes! You've accomplished the first task; the stage is set and you're off to day one. This may start tomorrow, or it may start after reading the next few lines but know that YOU can do this. You are a worthy investment, and you are worth the growth that will come from this book. God loves you; I love you, and you should love you. So, get ready to get started. My hope and prayer is that you'll see this journey as a benefit, and it will catapult you to the next dimension of your faith walk. If you need prayer or encouragement during this time, please email info@e2vproject.org. Our team will connect with you as needed throughout this journey. See, I'm already proving you are worth the investment!

DAY 1

BEGIN YOUR DAY...

◇ **Prayer**
Today, just set the stage, spend 5 minutes clearing your mind and totally focus in on God.

Bonus (Not Required) – Spend another 5 minutes simply thanking God for anything that comes to mind.

◇ **Bible Reading**
I am the Lord your God and I never change. – Malachi 3:6

Bonus (Not Required) – *I am full of mercy and grace and I overflow with love.* – Psalm 103:8

◇ **Devotional**
How has knowing that God never changes and that He is overflowing with love given you confidence and peace in your life? Think of this question throughout the day…

END YOUR DAY...

◇ **Journaling**
Write one sentence on an interaction, realization, or insight that impacted you today.

____

____

____

DAY 2

BEGIN YOUR DAY...

◇ **Prayer**

Today, just set the stage, spend 5 minutes clearing your mind and totally focus in on God.

Bonus (Not Required) – Spend another 5 minutes simply thanking God for anything that comes to mind.

◇ **Bible Reading**

The intentions of My heart will remain steadfast forever.
– Psalm 33:11

Bonus (Not Required) – *I created you in My own image with My special blessing.* – Genesis 1:27-28

◇ **Devotional**

How has the thought of you being created in God's image impacted you? Think of this question throughout the day…

END YOUR DAY...

◇ **Journaling**

Write one sentence on an interaction, realization, or insight that impacted you today.

____

____

____

DAY 3

BEGIN YOUR DAY...

◇ **Prayer**

Today, just set the stage, spend 5 minutes clearing your mind and totally focus in on God.

Bonus (Not Required) – Spend another 5 minutes simply thanking God for anything that comes to mind.

◇ **Bible Reading**

I chose you to be adopted into My family before creation.
– Ephesians 1:4-5

Bonus (Not Required) – *He delivered you from darkness into the kingdom of My beloved Son.* – Colossians 1:13

◇ **Devotional**

You are chosen by God; how does that make you feel?
Think of this question throughout the day...

END YOUR DAY...

◇ **Journaling**

Write one sentence on an interaction, realization, or insight that impacted you today.

DAY 4

BEGIN YOUR DAY...

◇ **Prayer**
Today, just set the stage, spend 5 minutes clearing your mind and totally focus in on God.

Bonus (Not Required) – Spend another 5 minutes simply thanking God for anything that comes to mind.

◇ **Bible Reading**
I have given you eternal life because you have believed in Jesus Christ. – John 3:16

Bonus (Not Required) – *I sent the Spirit of My Son into your heart so you could call Me Father.* – Galatians 4:6

◇ **Devotional**
How has accepting Jesus changed you? What's your favorite thing He's changed? Think of this question throughout the day…

END YOUR DAY...

◇ **Journaling**
Write one sentence on an interaction, realization, or insight that impacted you today.

____

____

____

DAY 5

BEGIN YOUR DAY...

◇ Prayer

Today, just set the stage, spend 5 minutes clearing your mind and totally focus in on God.

Bonus (Not Required) – Spend another 5 minutes simply thanking God for anything that comes to mind.

◇ Bible Reading

Since you are in Christ, I have made you an heir of all My promises. – Galatians 3:29

Bonus (Not Required) – *I have given you a new heart and put My own Spirit in you.* – Ezekiel 36:26-27

◇ Devotional

How does it make you feel that God wants to pour blessings on you? Think of this question throughout the day…

END YOUR DAY...

◇ Journaling

Write one sentence on an interaction, realization, or insight that impacted you today.

DAY 6

BEGIN YOUR DAY...

◇ **Prayer**

Today, just set the stage, spend 5 minutes clearing your mind and totally focus in on God.

Bonus (Not Required) – Spend another 5 minutes simply thanking God for anything that comes to mind.

◇ **Bible Reading**

My plan for your future is filled with hope. – Jeremiah 29:11

Bonus (Not Required) – *I am at work in your life through the desires of your heart.* – Philippians 2:13

◇ **Devotional**

How comforted are you knowing that God's plan for you leads to success? Think of this question throughout the day...

END YOUR DAY...

◇ **Journaling**

Write one sentence on an interaction, realization, or insight that impacted you today.

DAY 7

BEGIN YOUR DAY...

◇ **Prayer**

Today, just set the stage, spend 5 minutes clearing your mind and totally focus in on God.

Bonus (Not Required) – Spend another 5 minutes simply thanking God for anything that comes to mind.

◇ **Bible Reading**

I give My Spirit in unlimited measure. – John 3:34

Bonus (Not Required) – *I will take hold of your hand to keep you from falling.* – Psalm 37:24

◇ **Devotional**

Think of a time when God took hold of your hand when you were about to fall. Think of this question throughout the day…

END YOUR DAY...

◇ **Journaling**

Write one sentence on an interaction, realization, or insight that impacted you today.

____

____

____

DAY 8

BEGIN YOUR DAY...

◇ **Prayer**

Today, just set the stage, spend 5 minutes clearing your mind and totally focus in on God.

Bonus (Not Required) – Spend another 5 minutes simply thanking God for anything that comes to mind.

◇ **Bible Reading**

I will provide every good thing you need to do My will.
– Hebrews 13:20-21

Bonus (Not Required) – *I will discipline you in love, as a father who loves His children.* – Proverbs 3:11-12

◇ **Devotional**

Think of a time when God disciplined you. Was it as bad as you thought it would be? Think of this question throughout the day...

END YOUR DAY...

◇ **Journaling**

Write one sentence on an interaction, realization, or insight that impacted you today.

DAY 9

BEGIN YOUR DAY...

◇ **Prayer**

Today, just set the stage, spend 5 minutes clearing your mind and totally focus in on God.

Bonus (Not Required) – Spend another 5 minutes simply thanking God for anything that comes to mind.

◇ **Bible Reading**

My power will rest on you when you are weak. – 2 Corinthians 12:9

Bonus (Not Required) – *I will bless your life and keep watch over you always.* – Numbers 6:24

◇ **Devotional**

Are you comforted knowing that God is watching over you? Think of this question throughout the day…

END YOUR DAY...

◇ **Journaling**

Write one sentence on an interaction, realization, or insight that impacted you today.

____

____

____

DAY 10

BEGIN YOUR DAY...

◇ **Prayer**

Today, just set the stage, spend 5 minutes clearing your mind and totally focus in on God.

Bonus (Not Required) – Spend another 5 minutes simply thanking God for anything that comes to mind.

◇ **Bible Reading**

If you search for Me with all your heart, you will find me.
– Jeremiah 29:13

Bonus (Not Required) – *I will shield your life and deliver you from the wicked.* – Psalm 97:10

◇ **Devotional**

How do you feel knowing that if you seek God you will find Him? Think of this question throughout the day…

END YOUR DAY...

◇ **Journaling**

Write one sentence on an interaction, realization, or insight that impacted you today.

____

____

____

DAY 11

BEGIN YOUR DAY...

Prayer

Today, just set the stage, spend 5 minutes clearing your mind and totally focus in on God.

Bonus (Not Required) – Spend another 5 minutes simply thanking God for anything that comes to mind.

Bible Reading

Cast all your worries on Me, for I really care about you. – 1 Peter 5:7

I will not let you be tested beyond what you can endure.
– 1 Corinthians 10:13

Devotional

When is the last time you smiled knowing God cared for you? Think of this question throughout the day...

END YOUR DAY...

Journaling

Write one sentence on an interaction, realization, or insight that impacted you today.

DAY 12

BEGIN YOUR DAY...

◇ **Prayer**

Today, just set the stage, spend 5 minutes clearing your mind and totally focus in on God.

Bonus (Not Required) – Spend another 5 minutes simply thanking God for anything that comes to mind.

◇ **Bible Reading**

My love will persevere through every situation. – 1 Corinthians 13:4-7

I will not withhold anything good from those with an upright heart. – Psalm 84:11

◇ **Devotional**

How has God's unconditional love impacted how you love? Think of this question throughout the day...

END YOUR DAY...

◇ **Journaling**

Write one sentence on an interaction, realization, or insight that impacted you today.

____

____

____

DAY 13

BEGIN YOUR DAY...

Prayer

Today, just set the stage, spend 5 minutes clearing your mind and totally focus in on God.

Bonus (Not Required) – Spend another 5 minutes simply thanking God for anything that comes to mind.

Bible Reading

I look after foreigners and I help the fatherless and the widow. – Psalm 146:9

I will guard those who have a childlike heart. – Psalm 116:6

Devotional

How does it make you feel knowing that God is for all people? Think of this question throughout the day…

END YOUR DAY...

Journaling

Write one sentence on an interaction, realization, or insight that impacted you today.

DAY 14

BEGIN YOUR DAY...

◇ **Prayer**

Today, just set the stage, spend 5 minutes clearing your mind and totally focus in on God.

Bonus (Not Required) – Spend another 5 minutes simply thanking God for anything that comes to mind.

◇ **Bible Reading**

You are more than a conqueror through My love in Jesus Christ. – Romans 8:37

When Jesus appears, you will receive a crown of glory that will never dim. – 1 Peter 5:4

◇ **Devotional**

Think of a victorious life. Are you living one? Think of this question throughout the day…

END YOUR DAY...

◇ **Journaling**

Write one sentence on an interaction, realization, or insight that impacted you today.

DAY 15

BEGIN YOUR DAY...

Prayer

Today, just set the stage, spend 5 minutes clearing your mind and totally focus in on God.

Bonus (Not Required) – Spend another 5 minutes simply thanking God for anything that comes to mind.

Bible Reading

At the end of the age, my righteous ones will shine like the sun in My kingdom. – Matthew 13:43

Not one of My promises will ever fail you. – Joshua 23:14

Devotional

If God has promised it, do you believe you'll receive it? Think of this question throughout the day...

END YOUR DAY...

Journaling

Write one sentence on an interaction, realization, or insight that impacted you today.

DAY 16

BEGIN YOUR DAY...

Prayer

Today, just set the stage, spend 5 minutes clearing your mind and totally focus in on God.

Bonus (Not Required) – Spend another 5 minutes simply thanking God for anything that comes to mind.

Bible Reading

I am seated in the heavens and My kingdom reigns overall.
– Psalms 103:19

All My plans will be fulfilled, for I know the end from the beginning.
– Isaiah 46:10

Devotional

What does it mean to you when it's said, God is in control? Think of this question throughout the day…

END YOUR DAY...

Journaling

Write one sentence on an interaction, realization, or insight that impacted you today.

DAY
17

BEGIN YOUR DAY...

Prayer
Today, just set the stage, spend 5 minutes clearing your mind and totally focus in on God.

Bonus (Not Required) – Spend another 5 minutes simply thanking God for anything that comes to mind.

Bible Reading
I knew you before you were born, and I designed you for My purposes.
– Jeremiah 1:5

You are holy and free from blame because of Jesus Christ's death.
– Colossians 1:21-22

Devotional
Have your heard of a purpose driven life? Are you living yours? Think of this question throughout the day…

END YOUR DAY...

Journaling
Write one sentence on an interaction, realization, or insight that impacted you today.

DAY 18

BEGIN YOUR DAY...

◇ **Prayer**

Today, just set the stage, spend 5 minutes clearing your mind and totally focus in on God.

Bonus (Not Required) – Spend another 5 minutes simply thanking God for anything that comes to mind.

◇ **Bible Reading**

I have blotted out your sins and dissolved them like the mist.
– Isaiah 44:22

I have sealed you with My Spirit to guarantee your coming inheritance.
– Ephesians 1:13-14

◇ **Devotional**

God has forgiven your sins if you've asked. Have you forgiven yourself? Think of this question throughout the day…

END YOUR DAY...

◇ **Journaling**

Write one sentence on an interaction, realization, or insight that impacted you today.

DAY 19

BEGIN YOUR DAY...

◇ **Prayer**
Today, just set the stage, spend 5 minutes clearing your mind and totally focus in on God.

Bonus (Not Required) – Spend another 5 minutes simply thanking God for anything that comes to mind.

◇ **Bible Reading**
I will be a real Father to you. – 2 Corinthians 6:18

I will look after you and teach you the way that is best. – Psalm 32:8

◇ **Devotional**
How can God be a parent, friend, or companion to you? Think of this question throughout the day…

END YOUR DAY...

◇ **Journaling**
Write one sentence on an interaction, realization, or insight that impacted you today.

DAY 20

BEGIN YOUR DAY...

Prayer

Today, just set the stage, spend 5 minutes clearing your mind and totally focus in on God.

Bonus (Not Required) – Spend another 5 minutes simply thanking God for anything that comes to mind.

Bible Reading

Trust in Me with all your heart and I will guide you. – Proverbs 3:5-6

I will give you peace at all times and in every situation.
– 2 Thessalonians 3:16

Devotional

What's the hardest thing to trust God for? Think of this question throughout the day…

END YOUR DAY...

Journaling

Write one sentence on an interaction, realization, or insight that impacted you today.

DAY 21

BEGIN YOUR DAY...

◇ **Prayer**

Today, just set the stage, spend 5 minutes clearing your mind and totally focus in on God.

Bonus (Not Required) – Spend another 5 minutes simply thanking God for anything that comes to mind.

◇ **Bible Reading**

Call on Me when you are in trouble and I will rescue you.
– Psalm 91:15

I am your shelter and a place of safety from your enemies.
– Psalm 61:3

If you wait for Me, I will work on your behalf. – Isaiah 64:4

◇ **Devotional**

Is God your first call when you feeling troubled, sad, or overwhelmed? Think of this question throughout the day…

END YOUR DAY...

◇ **Journaling**

Write one sentence on an interaction, realization, or insight that impacted you today.

DAY 22

BEGIN YOUR DAY...

Prayer

Today, just set the stage, spend 5 minutes clearing your mind and totally focus in on God.

Bonus (Not Required) – Spend another 5 minutes simply thanking God for anything that comes to mind.

Bible Reading

My love will never fail you. – 1 Corinthians 13:8

I am your Shepherd and I will meet all your needs. – Psalm 23:1

I will keep you safe because no one can snatch you out of My hand. – John 10:29

Devotional

If God will meet your needs, what are you in need of that you haven't asked for? Think of this question throughout the day…

END YOUR DAY...

Journaling

Write one sentence on an interaction, realization, or insight that impacted you today.

DAY 23

BEGIN YOUR DAY...

Prayer

Today, just set the stage, spend 5 minutes clearing your mind and totally focus in on God.

Bonus (Not Required) – Spend another 5 minutes simply thanking God for anything that comes to mind.

Bible Reading

I will heal your broken heart and mend all your wounds. – Psalm 147:3

I will bless you in times of mourning with My comfort. – Matthew 5:4

You will find freedom wherever My Spirit dwells. – 2 Corinthians 3:17

Devotional

Are you brokenhearted about something? Have you asked God to heal you? Think of this question throughout the day…

END YOUR DAY...

Journaling

Write one sentence on an interaction, realization, or insight that impacted you today.

DAY 24

BEGIN YOUR DAY...

Prayer

Today, just set the stage, spend 5 minutes clearing your mind and totally focus in on God.

Bonus (Not Required) – Spend another 5 minutes simply thanking God for anything that comes to mind.

Bible Reading

You can know and depend on the love that I have for you.
– 1 John 4:16

You can trust in Me for I will never forsake you. – Psalm 9:10

I put people who are lonely in families. – Psalm 68:6

Devotional

Have you thought about and given God thanks for your extended family, the Church? Think of this question throughout the day...

END YOUR DAY...

Journaling

Write one sentence on an interaction, realization, or insight that impacted you today.

DAY 25

BEGIN YOUR DAY...

Prayer

Today, just set the stage, spend 5 minutes clearing your mind and totally focus in on God.

Bonus (Not Required) – Spend another 5 minutes simply thanking God for anything that comes to mind.

Bible Reading

I hear you when you ask for anything according to My will.
– 1 John 5:14

I will reward those who diligently seek Me with a heart of faith.
– Hebrews 11:6

I will sanctify you and keep you blameless until Jesus returns.
– 1 Thessalonians 5:23-24

Devotional

Are you purposefully seeking God? Have there been recent bumps in the road? Think of this question throughout the day…

END YOUR DAY...

Journaling

Write one sentence on an interaction, realization, or insight that impacted you today.

DAY 26

BEGIN YOUR DAY...

Prayer

Today, just set the stage, spend 5 minutes clearing your mind and totally focus in on God.

Bonus (Not Required) – Spend another 5 minutes simply thanking God for anything that comes to mind.

Bible Reading

When your body fails, you have an eternal home waiting for you.
– 2 Corinthians 5:1

Those who overcome will sit with My Son on His throne.
– Revelation 3:21

My promise of life is for you and for your family. – Acts 2:39

Devotional

What are your thoughts on death? Are you fearful of dying? Think of this question throughout the day…

END YOUR DAY...

Journaling

Write one sentence on an interaction, realization, or insight that impacted you today.

___

___

___

DAY
27

BEGIN YOUR DAY...

◇ **Prayer**
Today, just set the stage, spend 5 minutes clearing your mind and totally focus in on God.

Bonus (Not Required) – Spend another 5 minutes simply thanking God for anything that comes to mind.

◇ **Bible Reading**
All My promises are fulfilled in Christ. – 2 Corinthians 1:20

The earth belongs to Me and all that is in it. – Psalm 24:1

My throne will stand forever, and justice will reign in My kingdom. – Psalm 45:6

◇ **Devotional**
Do you really believe that God owns the earth? What does that mean to you? Think of this question throughout the day…

END YOUR DAY...

◇ **Journaling**
Write one sentence on an interaction, realization, or insight that impacted you today.

DAY 28

BEGIN YOUR DAY...

◇ **Prayer**
Today, just set the stage, spend 5 minutes clearing your mind and totally focus in on God.

Bonus (Not Required) – Spend another 5 minutes simply thanking God for anything that comes to mind.

◇ **Bible Reading**
The grass will dry up and flowers will fall, but My Word will endure forever. – 1 Peter 1:24-25

Though the mountains vanish, my unending love will never leave you. – Isaiah 54:10

I have called you out of darkness into My glorious light. – 1 Peter 2:9

◇ **Devotional**
If God's word never passes away, do you fully and completely trust it? Think of this question throughout the day…

END YOUR DAY...

◇ **Journaling**
Write one sentence on an interaction, realization, or insight that impacted you today.

____

____

____

DAY 29

BEGIN YOUR DAY...

Prayer

Today, just set the stage, spend 5 minutes clearing your mind and totally focus in on God.

Bonus (Not Required) – Spend another 5 minutes simply thanking God for anything that comes to mind.

Bible Reading

I have chosen the weak things of this world to confound the strong. – 1 Corinthians 1:27

I delight to reveal My kingdom to those with a childlike heart. – Matthew 11:25-26

I have brought you close through the blood of Christ. – Ephesians 2:13

Devotional

Think of a time when you were weak and God made you strong. Did you thank Him? Think of this question throughout the day...

END YOUR DAY...

Journaling

Write one sentence on an interaction, realization, or insight that impacted you today.

DAY 30

BEGIN YOUR DAY...

Prayer

Today, just set the stage, spend 5 minutes clearing your mind and totally focus in on God.

Bonus (Not Required) – Spend another 5 minutes simply thanking God for what anything that comes to mind.

Bible Reading

Your old life has died, and your new life is hid with Christ in Me.
– Colossians 3:3

The same Spirit that raised Jesus from the dead will also give life to you.
– Romans 8:11

I have blessed you in Christ with every heavenly blessing.
– Ephesians 1:3

Devotional

What has God created new in you? Do others see you different? Think of this question throughout the day…

END YOUR DAY...

Journaling

Write one sentence on an interaction, realization, or insight that impacted you today.

DAY 31

BEGIN YOUR DAY...

Prayer

Moving up to 10 minutes of prayer, spend 5 minutes clearing your mind and totally focus in on God. Now, spend another 5 minutes simply thanking God for anything that comes to mind.

Bible Reading

Commit all that you do to Me and your plans will be successful. – Proverbs 16:3

I am with you and I will help you because I am your God. – Isaiah 41:10

I will never abandon you. – Hebrews 13:5

Devotional

How does it make you feel knowing that God always has your back? Think of this question throughout the day…

END YOUR DAY...

Journaling

Write one sentence on an interaction, realization, or insight that impacted you today.

DAY 32

BEGIN YOUR DAY...

Prayer

In your 10 minutes of prayer, spend 5 minutes clearing your mind and totally focus in on God. Now, spend another 5 minutes simply thanking God for anything that comes to mind.

Bible Reading

I see all your hardships and I care about your suffering. – Psalm 31:7

When you pass through turbulent waters, I will be close to you. – Isaiah 43:2

My anointing will teach you all you need to know. – 1 John 2:27

Devotional

Have you been struggling with something lately? Have you taken it to God? Think of this question throughout the day…

END YOUR DAY...

Journaling

Write one sentence on an interaction, realization, or insight that impacted you today.

DAY 33

BEGIN YOUR DAY...

◇ **Prayer**

In your 10 minutes of prayer, spend 5 minutes clearing your mind and totally focus in on God. Now, spend another 5 minutes simply thanking God for anything that comes to mind.

◇ **Bible Reading**

If you live in My secret place, you will find rest under My shadow.
– Psalm 91:1

I will give you My strength to help you stand in high places.
– 2 Samuel 22:33-34

Thousands may fall around you, but you will not be harmed.
– Psalm 91:7

◇ **Devotional**

Do you know someone going through a tough time? Have you prayed God's blessing over them? Think of this question throughout the day…

END YOUR DAY...

◇ **Journaling**

Write one sentence on an interaction, realization, or insight that impacted you today.

DAY 34

BEGIN YOUR DAY...

Prayer

In your 10 minutes of prayer, spend 5 minutes clearing your mind and totally focus in on God. Now, spend another 5 minutes simply thanking God for anything that comes to mind.

Bible Reading

I provide food for the hungry and justice for the oppressed.
– Psalm 146:7

My divine power will give you all you need to live a good life.
– 2 Peter 1:3

My mercy will overrule judgment. – James 2:13

Devotional

Judgment is a sensitive thing. Has knowing God given you a different perspective on judgment and how you judge? Think of this question throughout the day…

END YOUR DAY...

Journaling

Write one sentence on an interaction, realization, or insight that impacted you today.

DAY 35

BEGIN YOUR DAY...

Prayer

In your 10 minutes of prayer, spend 5 minutes clearing your mind and totally focus in on God. Now, spend another 5 minutes simply thanking God for anything that comes to mind.

Bible Reading

I will cause all things to ultimately work for your good.
– Romans 8:28

Humble yourself before Me and in time I will exalt you. – 1 Peter 5:6

I have carved your name in the palms of My hands. – Isaiah 49:16

Devotional

Have you taken time to thank God for working things out for your good? Think of this question throughout the day…

END YOUR DAY...

Journaling

Write one sentence on an interaction, realization, or insight that impacted you today.

DAY
36

BEGIN YOUR DAY...

Prayer

In your 10 minutes of prayer, spend 5 minutes clearing your mind and totally focus in on God. Now, spend another 5 minutes simply thanking God for anything that comes to mind.

Bible Reading

Never tire of doing good, for in time you will reap a harvest.
– Galatians 6:9

An eternal crown awaits you at the finish line, so keep running your race. – 1 Corinthians 9:24-25

I prepared a kingdom inheritance for you when I created the world.
– Matthew 25:34

Devotional

Have you thought about your energy and confidence levels, knowing you are working on receiving an eternal crown at the end of your life here on Earth? Think of this question throughout the day…

END YOUR DAY...

Journaling

Write one sentence on an interaction, realization, or insight that impacted you today.

DAY 37

BEGIN YOUR DAY...

Prayer

In your 10 minutes of prayer, spend 5 minutes clearing your mind and totally focus in on God. Now, spend another 5 minutes simply thanking God for anything that comes to mind.

Bible Reading

It is precious for Me to see My faithful ones come home.
– Psalm 116:15

I will not forget My promises because I am a merciful God.
– Deuteronomy 4:31

My kingdom is everlasting, and My dominion will endure forever.
– Psalm 145:13

Devotional

Are you scared of death? Why? Think of this question throughout the day…

END YOUR DAY...

Journaling

Write one sentence on an interaction, realization, or insight that impacted you today.

DAY 38

BEGIN YOUR DAY...

Prayer

In your 10 minutes of prayer, spend 5 minutes clearing your mind and totally focus in on God. Now, spend another 5 minutes simply thanking God for anything that comes to mind.

Bible Reading

My eternal Word is anchored in the heavens. – Psalm 119:89

I am a gracious God who is righteous and full of mercy.
– Psalm 116:5

I created all things for My pleasure. – Revelation 4:11

Devotional

Have you sat back and thought about how a fully trustworthy God has spoken blessings and love over your life? Think of this question throughout the day…

END YOUR DAY...

Journaling

Write one sentence on an interaction, realization, or insight that impacted you today.

DAY 39

BEGIN YOUR DAY...

Prayer

In your 10 minutes of prayer, spend 5 minutes clearing your mind and totally focus in on God. Now, spend another 5 minutes simply thanking God for anything that comes to mind.

Bible Reading

I am your Father and you are My handiwork. – Isaiah 64:8

I will protect and carry you all the days of your life. – Isaiah 46:4

I have chosen you to be like My Son, so you could be part of My family. – Romans 8:29

Devotional

Sit back today and think of God as your Father. How does it make you feel? Think of this question throughout the day…

END YOUR DAY...

Journaling

Write one sentence on an interaction, realization, or insight that impacted you today.

DAY 40

BEGIN YOUR DAY...

Prayer

In your 10 minutes of prayer, spend 5 minutes clearing your mind and totally focus in on God. Now, spend another 5 minutes simply thanking God for anything that comes to mind.

Bible Reading

I have canceled all your sin and made you alive in Jesus Christ.
– Colossians 2:13-14

I have raised you up with Christ to sit in heavenly places.
– Ephesians 2:5-6

The good things that I have planned for you are too many to count.
– Psalm 40:5

Devotional

It's great to be debt-free as it pertains to the world, but what about debt-free to sin? Have you given thanks for that freedom lately? Think of this question throughout the day...

END YOUR DAY...

Journaling

Write one sentence on an interaction, realization, or insight that impacted you today.

DAY 41

BEGIN YOUR DAY...

Prayer

Moving up to 15 minutes of prayer, spend 5 minutes clearing your mind and totally focus in on God, spend 5 minutes thanking God, and now add 5 minutes praying over a friend or loved one. Keep it up! You're doing great!

Bible Reading

I will restore and refresh your weary soul. – Psalm 23:3

I will always build you up, not pull you down. – Jeremiah 24:6

I have made you a member of My own household. – Ephesians 2:19

Devotional

Where do you need refreshing? Are you willing to meditate on it today and give it to the Lord? Think of this question throughout the day…

END YOUR DAY...

Journaling

Write one sentence on an interaction, realization, or insight that impacted you today.

____

____

____

DAY 42

BEGIN YOUR DAY...

◇ **Prayer**

In your 15 minutes of prayer, spend 5 minutes clearing your mind and totally focus in on God, spend 5 minutes thanking God, and 5 minutes praying over a friend or loved one.

◇ **Bible Reading**

If you make your home in Me, then no evil will come your way.
– Psalm 91:9-10

If you delight in My Word, you will be fruitful and prosperous.
– Psalm 1:1-3

I will cover you all day long as you rest between My shoulders.
– Deuteronomy 33:12

◇ **Devotional**

When the Bible speaks of making you fruitful and prosperous, what does that mean to you? Think of this question throughout the day…

END YOUR DAY...

◇ **Journaling**

Write one sentence on an interaction, realization, or insight that impacted you today.

DAY 43

BEGIN YOUR DAY...

Prayer

In your 15 minutes of prayer, spend 5 minutes clearing your mind and totally focus in on God, spend 5 minutes thanking God, and 5 minutes praying over a friend or loved one.

Bible Reading

Come close to Me and I will come close to you. – James 4:8

You can trust in Me, for I am your strength and your song. – Isaiah 12:2

My gentleness will enlarge your life. – 2 Samuel 22:36

Devotional

What is one way that you can get closer to God? Think of this question throughout the day…

END YOUR DAY...

Journaling

Write one sentence on an interaction, realization, or insight that impacted you today.

DAY
44

BEGIN YOUR DAY...

◇ **Prayer**
In your 15 minutes of prayer, spend 5 minutes clearing your mind and totally focus in on God, spend 5 minutes thanking God, and 5 minutes praying over a friend or loved one.

◇ **Bible Reading**
I do not show favoritism in My family. – Ephesians 6:9

I have chosen the poor to be rich in faith and heirs of My kingdom. – James 2:5

Ask Me for wisdom and I will generously give it to you. – James 1:5

◇ **Devotional**
God says in His Word that he does not show favoritism. Do you? Think of this question throughout the day…

END YOUR DAY...

◇ **Journaling**
Write one sentence on an interaction, realization, or insight that impacted you today.

55

DAY
45

GIN YOUR DAY...

Prayer

In your 15 minutes of prayer, spend 5 minutes clearing your mind and totally focus in on God, spend 5 minutes thanking God, and 5 minutes praying over a friend or loved one.

Bible Reading

I will give you power to know the vastness of My immeasurable love. – Ephesians 3:17-19

Wait patiently for Me and I will hear your cry. – Psalm 40:1

Even when you are weak in your faith, I will remain faithful to you. – 2 Timothy 2:13

Devotional

God's love is truly immeasurable. How has believing this truth changed you? Think of this question throughout the day...

END YOUR DAY...

Journaling

Write one sentence on an interaction, realization, or insight that impacted you today.

DAY 46

BEGIN YOUR DAY...

◇ **Prayer**
In your 15 minutes of prayer, spend 5 minutes clearing your mind and totally focus in on God, spend 5 minutes thanking God, and 5 minutes praying over a friend or loved one.

◇ **Bible Reading**
Seek My kingdom first and everything you need will be given to you.
– Luke 12:31

My Spirit will lead you into all truth and show you what is to come.
– John 16:12-13

One day, I will wipe away every tear and take away all your pain.
– Revelation 21:4

◇ **Devotional**
If God's Spirit will lead you into all truth, how do you feel you are being led? Are you following that prompting? Think of this question throughout the day…

END YOUR DAY...

◇ **Journaling**
Write one sentence on an interaction, realization, or insight that impacted you today.

___

___

___

DAY 47

BEGIN YOUR DAY...

Prayer

In your 15 minutes of prayer, spend 5 minutes clearing your mind and totally focus in on God, spend 5 minutes thanking God, and 5 minutes praying over a friend or loved one.

Bible Reading

My everlasting joy and gladness will drive all sorrow and mourning away. – Isaiah 51:11

You can hold on to the hope that I will not change what I have promised. – Hebrews 6:17-18

My Spirit made you and My breath gives you life. – Job 33:4

Devotional

Do you see yourself as a more joyous person since you've come to know the Lord? Have you thanked Him for this blessing? Think of this question throughout the day...

END YOUR DAY...

Journaling

Write one sentence on an interaction, realization, or insight that impacted you today.

DAY
48

BEGIN YOUR DAY...

◇ **Prayer**
In your 15 minutes of prayer, spend 5 minutes clearing your mind and totally focus in on God, spend 5 minutes thanking God, and 5 minutes praying over a friend or loved one.

◇ **Bible Reading**
There is no place you can go to escape My presence. – Psalm 139:7-10

All your days are known to Me and your inheritance is secure forever. – Psalm 37:18

I gently formed you in your mother's womb. – Psalm 139:13

◇ **Devotional**
Are there areas in your life where you wish you could hide from God's presence? Are you ready to give those up and repent from holding onto them for so long? Think of this question throughout the day…

END YOUR DAY...

◇ **Journaling**
Write one sentence on an interaction, realization, or insight that impacted you today.

DAY
49

BEGIN YOUR DAY...

Prayer
In your 15 minutes of prayer, spend 5 minutes clearing your mind and totally focus in on God, spend 5 minutes thanking God, and 5 minutes praying over a friend or loved one.

Bible Reading
I am delighted to give you My kingdom. – Luke 12:32

My face will shine upon you all the days of your life. – Numbers 6:25

My Word will brighten your steps and light your path.
– Psalm 119:105

Devotional
God has promised repeatedly to be a light unto your path. Are you being a light for someone else who does not know the Lord? Think of this question throughout the day...

END YOUR DAY...

Journaling
Write one sentence on an interaction, realization, or insight that impacted you today.

DAY
50

BEGIN YOUR DAY...

◇ **Prayer**

In your 15 minutes of prayer, spend 5 minutes clearing your mind and totally focus in on God, spend 5 minutes thanking God, and 5 minutes praying over a friend or loved one.

◇ **Bible Reading**

My Son took upon Himself all your sicknesses and diseases.
– Matthew 8:16-17

My Spirit will help you in your weakness. – Romans 8:26

You can do all things through Jesus Christ who gives you strength.
– Philippians 4:13

◇ **Devotional**

Jesus paid for your healing. Healing comes in many ways; have you asked Him to heal an area in your life (spirit, mind, or body)? Think of this question throughout the day...

END YOUR DAY...

◇ **Journaling**

Write one sentence on an interaction, realization, or insight that impacted you today.

DAY 51

BEGIN YOUR DAY...

Prayer

Moving up to 20 minutes of prayer, spend 5 minutes for mental clarity, 5 minutes thanking God, 5 minutes for a friend or loved one, and now add 5 minutes for a need you have. Look at you go prayer warrior!

Bible Reading

Be courageous, for I am with you and I will never fail you. – Deuteronomy 31:6

I am a very present help for you in times of trouble. – Psalm 46:1

I will keep watch over you and guard you forever. – Psalm 12:7

Devotional

How can you be more courageous for the Lord? Think of this question throughout the day…

END YOUR DAY...

Journaling

Write one sentence on an interaction, realization, or insight that impacted you today.

DAY 52

BEGIN YOUR DAY...

Prayer

In your 20 minutes of prayer, spend 5 minutes for mental clarity, 5 minutes thanking God, 5 minutes for a friend or loved one, and 5 minutes for a need you have.

Bible Reading

I hear your voice when you call to Me in the morning. – Psalm 5:3

All that I have is yours because you belong to Jesus. – John 16:15

My goodness and mercy will chase after you all your life. – Psalm 23:6

Devotional

Do you take time to thank God when you first wake up? How has that changed your day? Does starting your day victoriously help you end your day victoriously? Think of this question throughout the day…

END YOUR DAY...

Journaling

Write one sentence on an interaction, realization, or insight that impacted you today.

DAY 53

BEGIN YOUR DAY...

Prayer

In your 20 minutes of prayer, spend 5 minutes for mental clarity, 5 minutes thanking God, 5 minutes for a friend or loved one, and 5 minutes for a need you have.

Bible Reading

I will teach your children My ways and give them great peace. – Isaiah 54:13

I will not forget the love you have shown Me by serving others. – Hebrews 6:10

I will repay those who are kind to the poor. – Proverbs 19:17

Devotional

What has the Lord been teaching you? Have you considered how it's made you a better person? Think of this question throughout the day...

END YOUR DAY...

Journaling

Write one sentence on an interaction, realization, or insight that impacted you today.

DAY 54

BEGIN YOUR DAY...

Prayer

In your 20 minutes of prayer, spend 5 minutes for mental clarity, 5 minutes thanking God, 5 minutes for a friend or loved one, and 5 minutes for a need you have.

Bible Reading

All My blessings will overtake those who obey Me.
– Deuteronomy 28:2

I know what you need before you even ask. – Matthew 6:8

I open prison doors and set captives free. – Isaiah 61:1

Devotional

If the Lord knows what you need before you even ask, why are you hesitating to ask Him? Why are you holding back? Think of this question throughout the day…

END YOUR DAY...

Journaling

Write one sentence on an interaction, realization, or insight that impacted you today.

DAY 55

BEGIN YOUR DAY...

Prayer

In your 20 minutes of prayer, spend 5 minutes for mental clarity, 5 minutes thanking God, 5 minutes for a friend or loved one, and 5 minutes for a need you have.

Bible Reading

I will rescue the godly from all their troubles. – 2 Peter 2:9

My displeasure may last a moment, but My favor is yours for life. – Psalm 30:5

I will fill those who hunger and thirst for My righteousness. – Matthew 5:6

Devotional

Are you still hanging your head in defeat after being corrected by the Lord? Why are you holding onto something that, if you've asked, He's forgiven you for? Forgive yourself! Think of this question throughout the day…

END YOUR DAY...

Journaling

Write one sentence on an interaction, realization, or insight that impacted you today.

DAY 56

BEGIN YOUR DAY...

◇ **Prayer**

In your 20 minutes of prayer, spend 5 minutes for mental clarity, 5 minutes thanking God, 5 minutes for a friend or loved one, and 5 minutes for a need you have.

◇ **Bible Reading**

I will show you the mysteries of My kingdom. – Matthew 13:11

Those who overcome will eat from the tree of life in paradise. – Revelation 2:7

I have prepared amazing things for those who love Me. – 1 Corinthians 2:9

◇ **Devotional**

What is one of those mysteries of God's Kingdom that you cannot wait to get an answer to? Why is it so mysterious to you? Does it help you ponder on God's greatness? Think of this question throughout the day…

END YOUR DAY...

◇ **Journaling**

Write one sentence on an interaction, realization, or insight that impacted you today.

DAY 57

BEGIN YOUR DAY...

Prayer

In your 20 minutes of prayer, spend 5 minutes for mental clarity, 5 minutes thanking God, 5 minutes for a friend or loved one, and 5 minutes for a need you have.

Bible Reading

Those who are pure in heart will see My face. – Matthew 5:8

I began the good work in you and I will finish it. – Philippians 1:6

You can rest in My promise of eternal life, for I cannot lie. – Titus 1:2

Devotional

What work has God started in you? Have you thanked Him for the progress lately? Think of this question throughout the day…

END YOUR DAY...

Journaling

Write one sentence on an interaction, realization, or insight that impacted you today.

DAY 58

BEGIN YOUR DAY...

◇ **Prayer**

In your 20 minutes of prayer, spend 5 minutes for mental clarity, 5 minutes thanking God, 5 minutes for a friend or loved one, and 5 minutes for a need you have.

◇ **Bible Reading**

My love is everlasting, and My faithfulness extends to all generations. – Psalm 100:5

My righteousness towers like the mountains and My justice goes deep as the sea. – Psalm 36:6

My Word will not return to Me until it accomplishes what I intended. – Isaiah 55:10-11

◇ **Devotional**

If God intends to accomplish what He's started in you, why do you try to hold Him back from doing it? Would you be free to give it up and give it all to Him? Think of this question throughout the day…

END YOUR DAY...

◇ **Journaling**

Write one sentence on an interaction, realization, or insight that impacted you today.

____

____

____

DAY 59

BEGIN YOUR DAY...

Prayer

In your 20 minutes of prayer, spend 5 minutes for mental clarity, 5 minutes thanking God, 5 minutes for a friend or loved one, and 5 minutes for a need you have.

Bible Reading

When I open My hand, I provide for all that I created. – Psalm 145:16

I love you as deeply as a father loves his children. – Psalm 103:13

I will not abandon you, for I am glad to make you My very own. – 1 Samuel 12:22

Devotional

God has made you His own. You've been adopted into His family. How can you show others this family? Is bringing someone to God important to you? Think of this question throughout the day…

END YOUR DAY...

Journaling

Write one sentence on an interaction, realization, or insight that impacted you today.

DAY 60

BEGIN YOUR DAY...

Prayer

In your 20 minutes of prayer, spend 5 minutes for mental clarity, 5 minutes thanking God, 5 minutes for a friend or loved one, and 5 minutes for a need you have.

Bible Reading

My lovingkindness is more precious than life. – Psalm 63:3

I made you holy by the once for all sacrifice of My Son, Jesus Christ. – Hebrews 10:10

I have removed your sins from you as far as the east is from the west. – Psalm 103:12

Devotional

Is your relationship with Christ more precious than anything else in life? Is that thought foreign to you? Have you sat and really pondered it? Is the Lord really number one? Think of this question throughout the day…

END YOUR DAY...

Journaling

Write one sentence on an interaction, realization, or insight that impacted you today.

DAY 61

BEGIN YOUR DAY...

Prayer

In your 20 minutes of prayer, spend 5 minutes for mental clarity, 5 minutes thanking God, 5 minutes for a friend or loved one, and 5 minutes for a need you have.

Bible Reading

You can enjoy freedom because Christ has set you free. – Galatians 5:1

I have anointed you with My Spirit as a down payment of what is yet to come. – 2 Corinthians 1:21-22

Every good gift that you receive comes directly from My hand. – James 1:17

Devotional

If your life in Christ is good now, can you even imagine what God has yet to come for you? Think of this question throughout the day...

END YOUR DAY...

Journaling

Write two sentences on an interaction, realization, or insight that impacted you today.

DAY
62

BEGIN YOUR DAY...

Prayer
In your 20 minutes of prayer, spend 5 minutes for mental clarity, 5 minutes thanking God, 5 minutes for a friend or loved one, and 5 minutes for a need you have.

Bible Reading
Nothing will be impossible for those who have even a little faith.
– Matthew 17:19-20

Call out to Me and I will show you wonderful things you do not know.
– Jeremiah 33:3

I will reveal My secrets to those who fear Me. – Psalm 25:14

Devotional
What did you find impossible before, but now serving Christ and having faith it is no longer impossible? Think of this question throughout the day…

END YOUR DAY...

Journaling
Write two sentences on an interaction, realization, or insight that impacted you today.

DAY 63

BEGIN YOUR DAY...

Prayer
In your 20 minutes of prayer, spend 5 minutes for mental clarity, 5 minutes thanking God, 5 minutes for a friend or loved one, and 5 minutes for a need you have.

Bible Reading
I am able to do more for you than you could possibly imagine.
– Ephesians 3:20

When you walk through the fires of adversity, you will not be burned.
– Isaiah 43:2

No weapon created for your harm will succeed against you.
– Isaiah 54:17

Devotional
How has your confidence grown knowing God is your protector? Think of this question throughout the day...

END YOUR DAY...

Journaling
Write two sentences on an interaction, realization, or insight that impacted you today.

DAY
64

BEGIN YOUR DAY...

◇ **Prayer**
In your 20 minutes of prayer, spend 5 minutes for mental clarity, 5 minutes thanking God, 5 minutes for a friend or loved one, and 5 minutes for a need you have.

◇ **Bible Reading**
I will give you a garment of praise in exchange for your spirit of heaviness. – Isaiah 61:3

My Spirit will rest on you when you suffer for Christ's sake. – 1 Peter 4:14

My goodness will lead you to a change of heart. – Romans 2:4

◇ **Devotional**
What have you exchanged in your life with Jesus, and are amazed at the outcome? Think of this question throughout the day…

END YOUR DAY...

◇ **Journaling**
Write two sentences on an interaction, realization, or insight that impacted you today.

DAY 65

BEGIN YOUR DAY...

◇ **Prayer**

In your 20 minutes of prayer, spend 5 minutes for mental clarity, 5 minutes thanking God, 5 minutes for a friend or loved one, and 5 minutes for a need you have.

◇ **Bible Reading**

I will bless the peacemakers and call them My children. – Matthew 5:9

I will protect the fatherless, and widows can trust in Me.
– Jeremiah 49:11

I will provide justice for everyone who is mistreated. – Psalm 103:6

◇ **Devotional**

Peacefulness is a process. How are you working to make your life more peaceful? Think of this question throughout the day…

END YOUR DAY...

◇ **Journaling**

Write two sentences on an interaction, realization, or insight that impacted you today.

DAY 66

BEGIN YOUR DAY...

Prayer
In your 20 minutes of prayer, spend 5 minutes for mental clarity, 5 minutes thanking God, 5 minutes for a friend or loved one, and 5 minutes for a need you have.

Bible Reading
My name is a strong tower that you can run to and find safety.
– Proverbs 18:10

When you leave your body, you will be at home in My presence.
– 2 Corinthians 5:8

The world and its passions will disappear, but those who do My will shall live forever. – 1 John 2:17

Devotional
When is the last time you really cranked up the praise for God's protection over you? Think of this question throughout the day…

END YOUR DAY...

Journaling
Write two sentences on an interaction, realization, or insight that impacted you today.

DAY 67

BEGIN YOUR DAY...

Prayer

In your 20 minutes of prayer, spend 5 minutes for mental clarity, 5 minutes thanking God, 5 minutes for a friend or loved one, and 5 minutes for a need you have.

Bible Reading

I will rescue you from evil and safely deliver you into My kingdom. – 2 Timothy 4:18

There is a crown of righteousness waiting for everyone who loves My Son. – 2 Timothy 4:8

If you persist and do My will, you will receive what I have promised. – Hebrews 10:36

Devotional

What does evil look like in your life? Identifying the enemy will help you combat it. Think of this question throughout the day…

END YOUR DAY...

Journaling

Write two sentences on an interaction, realization, or insight that impacted you today.

DAY 68

BEGIN YOUR DAY...

Prayer

In your 20 minutes of prayer, spend 5 minutes for mental clarity, 5 minutes thanking God, 5 minutes for a friend or loved one, and 5 minutes for a need you have.

Bible Reading

I made the heavens by My Word and I breathed the stars into existence. – Psalm 33:6

I am faithful to keep My covenant of kindness to a thousand generations. – Deuteronomy 7:9

All of mankind can find protection in the shadow of My wings. – Psalm 36:7

Devotional

God says ALL of mankind can find protection in Him. Does that help you gauge how BIG God really is? Think of this question throughout the day…

END YOUR DAY...

Journaling

Write two sentences on an interaction, realization, or insight that impacted you today.

DAY 69

BEGIN YOUR DAY...

Prayer

In your 20 minutes of prayer, spend 5 minutes for mental clarity, 5 minutes thanking God, 5 minutes for a friend or loved one, and 5 minutes for a need you have.

Bible Reading

I am a father to the fatherless and I defend the cause of widows. – Psalm 68:5

I will not abandon My own inheritance. – Psalm 94:14

I am the Lord your God who heals all of your diseases. – Exodus 15:26

Devotional

Think of a person you've lost. How has God filled that gap? Have you asked Him to fill it? Think of this question throughout the day…

END YOUR DAY...

Journaling

Write two sentences on an interaction, realization, or insight that impacted you today.

DAY 70

BEGIN YOUR DAY...

Prayer

In your 20 minutes of prayer, spend 5 minutes for mental clarity, 5 minutes thanking God, 5 minutes for a friend or loved one, and 5 minutes for a need you have.

Bible Reading

My love for you will last forever. – Jeremiah 31:3

I give good gifts to My children when they ask. – Matthew 7:11

Jesus is not ashamed to be called your big brother. – Hebrews 2:11

Devotional

How does it make you feel when God says, "My love for you will last forever?" Think of this question throughout the day…

END YOUR DAY...

Journaling

Write two sentences on an interaction, realization, or insight that impacted you today.

DAY 71

BEGIN YOUR DAY...

Prayer
In your 20 minutes of prayer, spend 5 minutes for mental clarity, 5 minutes thanking God, 5 minutes for a friend or loved one, and 5 minutes for a need you have.

Bible Reading
I forgive sins and I love to show mercy. – Micah 7:18

I have poured My love into your heart through My Spirit. – Romans 5:5

I have put My law within you and have written it on your heart. – Jeremiah 31:33

Devotional
How do you think you are doing following His laws and sharing His love? Think of this question throughout the day…

DAY 71 *continued*

END YOUR DAY...

Journaling

Write a paragraph on an interaction, realization, or insight that impacted you today.

DAY 72

BEGIN YOUR DAY...

Prayer

In your 20 minutes of prayer, spend 5 minutes for mental clarity, 5 minutes thanking God, 5 minutes for a friend or loved one, and 5 minutes for a need you have.

Bible Reading

I will meet your every need through My eternal riches in Jesus Christ. – Philippians 4:19

I will shepherd My inheritance and carry them forever. – Psalm 28:9

Do not be sad, for My joy is your strength. – Nehemiah 8:10

Devotional

When you are sad, do you call on God to bring joy into your life through His strength? Think of this question throughout the day…

DAY 72 *continued*

END YOUR DAY...

Journaling

Write a paragraph on an interaction, realization, or insight that impacted you today.

DAY 73

BEGIN YOUR DAY...

Prayer
In your 20 minutes of prayer, spend 5 minutes for mental clarity, 5 minutes thanking God, 5 minutes for a friend or loved one, and 5 minutes for a need you have.

Bible Reading
My perfect love will banish fear from your heart. – 1 John 4:18

I will save you in the midst of your troubles. – Psalm 138:7

I will blanket My protection over all who trust in Me. – Psalm 5:11

Devotional
Fear Meter Test: How are you handling things you fear? Are you allowing God to help cast out fear in your life? Think of this question throughout the day…

DAY
73
continued

END YOUR DAY...

Journaling

Write a paragraph on an interaction, realization, or insight that impacted you today.

DAY 74

BEGIN YOUR DAY...

Prayer

In your 20 minutes of prayer, spend 5 minutes for mental clarity, 5 minutes thanking God, 5 minutes for a friend or loved one, and 5 minutes for a need you have.

Bible Reading

My armor will help you stand against the plans of the enemy. – Ephesians 6:11

I will turn your mourning into dancing and surround you with joy. – Psalm 30:11

I will restore your health and heal all your hurts. – Jeremiah 30:17

Devotional

Have you checked your armor? What areas need worked on? Think of this question throughout the day...

DAY 74 *continued*

END YOUR DAY...

Journaling
Write a paragraph on an interaction, realization, or insight that impacted you today.

DAY
75

BEGIN YOUR DAY...

Prayer

In your 20 minutes of prayer, spend 5 minutes for mental clarity, 5 minutes thanking God, 5 minutes for a friend or loved one, and 5 minutes for a need you have.

Bible Reading

I will strengthen you with feet like a deer so you can reach great heights.
– Habakkuk 3:19

If you share with the needy, my glory will guard your back.
– Isaiah 58:7-8

If you enter into My rest, you will find rest from all your striving.
– Hebrews 4:9-10

Devotional

Since you started walking with Christ do you feel you've reached new heights? How? Think of this question throughout the day...

DAY 75 *continued*

END YOUR DAY...

◇ **Journaling**

Write a paragraph on an interaction, realization, or insight that impacted you today.

DAY 76

BEGIN YOUR DAY...

◇ **Prayer**

In your 20 minutes of prayer, spend 5 minutes for mental clarity, 5 minutes thanking God, 5 minutes for a friend or loved one, and 5 minutes for a need you have.

◇ **Bible Reading**

I am near to you whenever you cry out. – Deuteronomy 4:7

When problems arise, call to Me and I will answer you. – Psalm 86:7

Don't worry, I will take care of you. – Matthew 6:25-26

◇ **Devotional**

First Call Check-In: Do you go to God first when problems arise? Think of this question throughout the day...

DAY 76 *continued*

END YOUR DAY...

◇ **Journaling**

Write a paragraph on an interaction, realization, or insight that impacted you today.

DAY 77

BEGIN YOUR DAY...

Prayer

In your 20 minutes of prayer, spend 5 minutes for mental clarity, 5 minutes thanking God, 5 minutes for a friend or loved one, and 5 minutes for a need you have.

Bible Reading

Those who overcome will be pillars in My temple forever. – Revelation 3:12

You are My children now and you will be just like Jesus when He appears. – 1 John 3:2

One day, you will see My face and My name will be on your forehead. – Revelation 22:4

Devotional

Are you an overcomer? Have you told someone your story? Who could you tell your story to? Think of this question throughout the day...

DAY 77 *continued*

END YOUR DAY...

Journaling

Write a paragraph on an interaction, realization, or insight that impacted you today.

DAY 78

BEGIN YOUR DAY...

Prayer

In your 20 minutes of prayer, spend 5 minutes for mental clarity, 5 minutes thanking God, 5 minutes for a friend or loved one, and 5 minutes for a need you have.

Bible Reading

Every promise that I make is true, for I do not lie or change My mind. – Numbers 23:19

The heavens declare My glory and reveal My handiwork. – Psalm 19:1

I rule the earth and all the kings belong to Me. – Psalm 47:7-9

Devotional

How much more confidence do you have knowing that God is truthful, does not lie, or change His mind? Have you thanked Him for that? Think of this question throughout the day...

DAY 78 *continued*

END YOUR DAY...

Journaling

Write a paragraph on an interaction, realization, or insight that impacted you today.

DAY 79

BEGIN YOUR DAY...

◇ **Prayer**

In your 20 minutes of prayer, spend 5 minutes for mental clarity, 5 minutes thanking God, 5 minutes for a friend or loved one, and 5 minutes for a need you have.

◇ **Bible Reading**

You can trust in My faithfulness because My Word is true. – Psalm 33:4

I am good, and My mercy is everlasting. – 1 Chronicles 16:34

I have cared for you from the moment you were born. – Psalm 71:6

◇ **Devotional**

If God's mercy is everlasting, how is yours? Are you being merciful to people? Do you need to show someone a little more grace and mercy? Think of this question throughout the day…

DAY 79 *continued*

END YOUR DAY...

Journaling

Write a paragraph on an interaction, realization, or insight that impacted you today.

DAY 80

BEGIN YOUR DAY...

Prayer
In your 20 minutes of prayer, spend 5 minutes for mental clarity, 5 minutes thanking God, 5 minutes for a friend or loved one, and 5 minutes for a need you have.

Bible Reading
I have even numbered each hair on your head. – Matthew 10:30

Through faith in Christ, you can boldly approach Me with confidence. – Ephesians 3:12

If you walk in the light, the blood of My Son Jesus will cleanse you from all sin. – 1 John 1:7

Devotional
If God even knows the number of hairs on your head, what are you worried about? When will you get rid of those things that cause you worry? Think of this question throughout the day…

DAY 80 *continued*

END YOUR DAY...

◇ **Journaling**

Write a paragraph on an interaction, realization, or insight that impacted you today.

DAY 81

BEGIN YOUR DAY...

Prayer

In your 20 minutes of prayer, spend 5 minutes for mental clarity, 5 minutes thanking God, 5 minutes for a friend or loved one, and 5 minutes for a need you have.

Bible Reading

Trust in Me, and do not be afraid of what others can do to you.
– Psalm 56:11

I will be your security and a safe place for your children.
– Proverbs 14:26

I am your shield, your glory, and the lifter of your head. – Psalm 3:3

Read James 1

Devotional

Do you think you've been growing over these last few months? If so, what are 5 new things you can thank the Lord for? Think of this question throughout the day…

DAY
81
continued

END YOUR DAY...

Journaling
Write a paragraph on an interaction, realization, or insight that impacted you today.

DAY 82

BEGIN YOUR DAY...

Prayer

In your 20 minutes of prayer, spend 5 minutes for mental clarity, 5 minutes thanking God, 5 minutes for a friend or loved one, and 5 minutes for a need you have.

Bible Reading

I will gladly give the Holy Spirit to those who will ask. – Luke 11:13

Forgiveness and healing are among My many benefits.
– Psalm 103:2-3

If you rest in Me and wait patiently, you will inherit the land.
– Psalm 37:7-9

Read James 2

Devotional

Are you craving the move of the Holy Spirit more in your life? Have you quieted your heart to hear His prompting? Think of this question throughout the day…

DAY 82 *continued*

END YOUR DAY...

Journaling
Write a paragraph on an interaction, realization, or insight that impacted you today.

DAY 83

BEGIN YOUR DAY...

◇ **Prayer**

In your 20 minutes of prayer, spend 5 minutes for mental clarity, 5 minutes thanking God, 5 minutes for a friend or loved one, and 5 minutes for a need you have.

◇ **Bible Reading**

I give power to the exhausted and I strengthen the weak.
– Isaiah 40:29

If I am for you, no one can stand against you. – Romans 8:31

Though you have many plans, my purpose will be fulfilled.
– Proverbs 19:21

Read James 3

◇ **Devotional**

Are you feeling tired or worn out lately? Have you stopped and patiently waited on the Lord to renew you? Would taking a break hurt you? Think of this question throughout the day...

DAY
83
continued

END YOUR DAY...

Journaling
Write a paragraph on an interaction, realization, or insight that impacted you today.

DAY 84

BEGIN YOUR DAY...

Prayer

In your 20 minutes of prayer, spend 5 minutes for mental clarity, 5 minutes thanking God, 5 minutes for a friend or loved one, and 5 minutes for a need you have.

Bible Reading

If two of you agree in prayer, I will do whatever you ask. – Matthew 18:19

I will make you fruitful in your old age. – Psalm 92:13-14

Do not despise My discipline, for in time, I will heal your wounds. – Job 5:17-18

Read James 4

Devotional

Do you have an accountability partner? Do you have a prayer partner? Have you been in agreement in prayer with someone's need or a need of your own? Think of this question throughout the day...

DAY 84 *continued*

END YOUR DAY...

Journaling

Write a paragraph on an interaction, realization, or insight that impacted you today.

DAY 85

BEGIN YOUR DAY...

Prayer

In your 20 minutes of prayer, spend 5 minutes for mental clarity, 5 minutes thanking God, 5 minutes for a friend or loved one, and 5 minutes for a need you have.

Bible Reading

I bind up the brokenhearted and I will comfort all who mourn. – Isaiah 61:1-2

I will comfort you just like a mother would. – Isaiah 66:13

Your sadness may last for a night, but joy will come in the morning. – Psalm 30:5

Read James 5

Devotional

When is the last time you got alone with God and praised Him deeply for His comforting love? Think of this question throughout the day...

DAY 85 *continued*

END YOUR DAY...

Journaling
Write a paragraph on an interaction, realization, or insight that impacted you today.

DAY 86

BEGIN YOUR DAY...

Prayer

In your 20 minutes of prayer, spend 5 minutes for mental clarity, 5 minutes thanking God, 5 minutes for a friend or loved one, and 5 minutes for a need you have.

Bible Reading

I am pleased when you share with others. – Hebrews 13:16

I will keep you safe from the evil one. – 1 John 5:18

I will show mercy to those who are merciful to others. – Matthew 5:7

Read 1 John 1

Devotional

As you've developed your life in Christ, how has it changed how you personally deal with those who may not treat you well? Think of this question throughout the day...

DAY 86 *continued*

END YOUR DAY...

◇ **Journaling**
Write a paragraph on an interaction, realization, or insight that impacted you today.

DAY 87

BEGIN YOUR DAY...

Prayer

In your 20 minutes of prayer, spend 5 minutes for mental clarity, 5 minutes thanking God, 5 minutes for a friend or loved one, and 5 minutes for a need you have.

Bible Reading

I bless My righteous ones and shield them with My favor. – Psalm 5:12

I will anoint you with oil so your cup overflows. – Psalm 23:5

You can celebrate because your name is written in heaven. – Luke 10:20

Read 1 John 2

Devotional

Thinking of God's favor, how does it make you feel knowing you are one of His favorites? Think of this question throughout the day…

DAY
87
continued

END YOUR DAY...

◇ **Journaling**

Write a paragraph on an interaction, realization, or insight that impacted you today.

DAY 88

BEGIN YOUR DAY...

Prayer

In your 20 minutes of prayer, spend 5 minutes for mental clarity, 5 minutes thanking God, 5 minutes for a friend or loved one, and 5 minutes for a need you have.

Bible Reading

There is a special room in My house prepared just for you. – John 14:2

You can look forward to the new heaven and earth that I have promised. – 2 Peter 3:13

I spoke the universe into existence. – Genesis 1:1

Read 1 John 3

Devotional

When the Bible speaks of Heaven, what do you think about? Have you allowed yourself to dream about Heaven? How does it make you feel? Think of this question throughout the day...

DAY 88 *continued*

END YOUR DAY...

Journaling
Write a paragraph on an interaction, realization, or insight that impacted you today.

DAY 89

BEGIN YOUR DAY...

Prayer

In your 20 minutes of prayer, spend 5 minutes for mental clarity, 5 minutes thanking God, 5 minutes for a friend or loved one, and 5 minutes for a need you have.

Bible Reading

I give life and breath to all things. – Acts 17:24-25

You can rest in My love, for I have power to save you.
– Zephaniah 3:17

My thoughts toward you outnumber the sand on the seashore.
– Psalm 139:17-18

Read 1 John 4

Devotional

Stop what you are doing sometime today and recognize that God is completely head over heels for you. Can you list out 5 things that you can give Him praise for? Think of this question throughout the day…

DAY 89 *continued*

END YOUR DAY...

Journaling

Write a paragraph on an interaction, realization, or insight that impacted you today.

DAY 90

BEGIN YOUR DAY...

Prayer

In your 20 minutes of prayer, spend 5 minutes for mental clarity, 5 minutes thanking God, 5 minutes for a friend or loved one, and 5 minutes for a need you have.

Bible Reading

All the days of your life are written in My special book.
– Psalm 139:16

I will carry you in My arms just like a father carries his child.
– Deuteronomy 1:31

I will give you a double portion of your inheritance in exchange for your shame. – Isaiah 61:7

Read 1 John 5

Devotional

You've made it to the last day of this 90-day book. What are you going to do for day 91? How has this equipped you to have prayer, Bible reading, and a devotion regularly in your life? Take some time to think through this and what tomorrow will look like. Think of this question throughout the day…

DAY 90 *continued*

END YOUR DAY...

◇ **Journaling**

Write a paragraph on an interaction, realization, or insight that impacted you today.

IN CONCLUSION

I wanted to take a few minutes and add a few concluding thoughts that I believe will help you develop long term success in your walk with God. It is so important to know that roadblocks and lulls happen to everyone. Do not get discouraged if you "messed up" or missed a day or two. It takes time and as John Maxwell said, "Everything worthwhile is uphill and you cannot go uphill with downhill habits." So, in this last part of the book I want to give you some insight should you start to feel stuck in the areas of prayer, Bible reading, devotional, or journaling. Along with these are two other sections to conclude this book: the importance of mentoring and my personal story.

WHEN I AM STUCK...

WITH PRAYER

What I have always found useful is to stop what I am doing. Generally, when I am having trouble praying, I am way too busy. Find a quiet place - it does not need to be anywhere special, but a place where you will not be distracted. Also, leave your cell phone somewhere else. Calls, texts, social media, and games can wait for a few minutes. Now get quiet, set a goal for absolute silence for five minutes. When you feel your mind drifting, bring it back to center on the quietness. Once you have made it five minutes, take time to start firing as fast as you can all the things you are grateful for that God has given you - spouse, children, a job, a great church, etc. - you get the picture. If it feels fun, it is supposed to, praying should not be a chore or a bore, but joyous and fun. Now, once you have exhausted yourself of options, thank the Lord for a few minutes and then wait patiently and quietly in His presence. It may not happen overnight but after a few times using this method, you should find yourself back in steady communion with God.

WITH BIBLE READING

Nothing makes the enemy happier than when we stop reading God's Word. It is our lifeblood and our most trusted guide in this world. If we get weak here, we get weak everywhere else. To help combat this, try and find a favorite book of the Bible that you feel you could read many times and it would never get old (it won't anyway because it's the Living Word). What I have found helpful for me, is to go back to the Book of Psalms when I am feeling deflated or when I do not feel like getting into the Word that day (yes, it happens to all of us). The great thing is that Psalms highlights so much human emotion that flipping through a few pages can automatically help bring you back into focus. And while you are at it, you are reading the Word, double bonus. So, find a favorite; maybe you like stories of King David, or the Prophet Elijah. Go back and read the stories. It is all about consistency and setting a pattern, it does not mean you always have to read something new.

WITH DEVOTIONALS

Remember, highlighted in this book is the fact that devotion is the act of dedication to something. In our case, and with the direction of this book, it is taking core thoughts that we picked up along the way and thought on for a while, to see what God is saying to us on how to apply it to our everyday lives. So, maybe you are on a day or a few days when things just do not click, my suggestion is to go back to something that energized you and build upon that. Again, we are working towards consistency and not necessarily new material every day. Let me just say this now, your pace and your comfort are directly related to your relationship with God. The devotional is a helper, it is not the be-all-end-all. Trust yourself, be consistent and you will grow.

WITH JOURNALING

Okay, I get it, writing your thoughts down can be a challenging task to do daily - especially when we all have busy lives, but I assure you it is worth it. I have been journaling for years every day and I can honestly tell you, my walk with the Lord is closer and more solid than ever before. So, what do you do when you feel stuck? Start back over! Go back to writing one sentence, or two sentences. You do not have to write a novel - do not pressure yourself into doing so. Take time to think about one thing, that's it, one thing that happened today that you are happy about, pleased with, or brought you peace. Your journal entry may look like this: Lord, thank you for letting me wake up today, it was a tough one today, but I am thankful to be alive. Doesn't sound too hard, does it? I know I sound like a broken record, but you are driving for consistency not perfection.

WHY MENTORING IS IMPORTANT

I said earlier that I would plead my case on the importance of mentoring, so here it is - please be teachable and moldable. Learn to humble yourself and ask for help from someone who has been down the path before you and could be on their way back from the journey. When you choose to ask for coaching or mentoring you are catapulting yourself ahead in your journey. Asking for help or guidance could save you time, and not just a few minutes, it could save you years on achieving your goals. For example, before my dad passed in 2018, he and I were best friends. I could go to him about anything and because he had been down the path already, I was able to make up a lot of ground in my journey by taking his advice. I am glad I learned that parents do have pretty good answers sometimes and their hearts are to help their children. Thanks Dad, for all the love and advice along the way.

Mentors also have nothing to lose with you - meaning they can be as honest and straight forward as necessary and that could be a great thing for you moving forward. Something to do with this in mind is find someone who is sold out on prayer and ask if you can shadow them a few times when they are praying. Review how they pray and think about what areas you are struggling in, then sit back and listen to the advice they are offering to help you grow. Your next step is to follow the advice. Too many times we hear what we are to do, but do not take the action to do it. If you want to accomplish your goal, seek mentors, seek advice, listen for answers, and then act upon it.

MY STORY

I want to finish off this book by providing you a little more detail into my life and what I am all about. I am hoping by the simplicity of my writing and the simple, yet challenging goals I set before you in this book, that you see me as a person that is down to earth and a strong believer in not over complicating my faith walk with the Lord.

In January 1993, I thought I would take advantage of this overzealous youth pastor who offered to take me to McDonald's for lunch and a chat. I was thinking to myself, free lunch, and dessert, and out the door I would go. Little did I know that this lunch would change my life forever, literally! It was Revelation 3:20 that got me. God was standing at the door of my heart and wanted to come in and make a family with me. I come from a divorced home, both my parents are great, but something told me that this acceptance would be the answer and completeness I was looking for. I told the pastor I would humbly like to accept Christ into my heart, and he led me in a prayer. I do not remember the words, but I remember the feeling. What a sense of peace and joy. I have never forgotten that feeling. I admit I do not feel that way everyday or most days for that matter, but I know what I received was real and it was permanent.

Flash forwards a few years and yes, it is 2020, so I fully understand how far we are flashing forward, thank you very much. My journey has had many ups and downs. In fact, if my life were a real-life roller coaster, people would be in line for miles to ride it. Big ups, and big downs, corkscrews, and all. I am the first person to tell you that I am grateful for God's mercy and grace, because Lord knows I need it. What I am simply trying to say is that this walk is not easy, nor do I believe it was ever going to be after the fall in the garden by Adam and Eve. What I am trying to tell you is this is worth the effort and energy because God is simply the greatest thing you can encounter on Earth. I cannot even begin to imagine how awesome Heaven will be when we are in His presence.

Today, I get the privilege to lead a congregation in whom I love dearly. I have been the lead pastor for many years. I am the first person to tell you that longevity and tenure in the same location to minister is absolutely the best. I have seen kids come from youth groups to lead ministries and babies turn into teenagers. Is it worth it? Every minute. I pray that I get many more years with my church family, because they make me happy and Kingdom-minded every day. I can only hope and pray that you feel the same way about your church family. If you do, count it all as joy because you truly have an asset that many people do not.

I close with this. I pray for anyone reading this book that this is simply a starting block or a reset point to a great journey ahead. It is worth it, and you are worth it. You may have to start and restart, and to that I say, good, keep going. God loves you and truly loves the effort you make to give Him higher praise.

Blessings!